EAT SEX DATE

In the State of Singlehood Throw Out Dating

My Recipes to Get & Keep a "Good Value Man"

DEDICATION

This book is dedicated to my late grandmother, whom everyone said that I took after. I took her smile, her poise, her elegance, her style, and her beauty. She left the earth too soon to watch me grow into a mirror image of her.

ACKNOWLEDGMENTS

I would like to acknowledge the man who made it possible for me to love on purpose. He has been loving, supportive, and caring.

Contents

FOREWORD vii

CHAPTER 1: THE STATE OF SINGLEHOOD 1

CHAPTER 2: IT'S A MATCH 3

CHAPTER 3: THE 3-DATE RULE 7

CHAPTER 4: HE CALLED 9

CHAPTER 5: MY RECIPES 11

CHAPTER 6: SPICE THINGS UP 37

CHAPTER 7: THE CHANGE 41

CHAPTER 8: EAT, SEX, AND DATE 43

CHAPTER 9: SAY MY NAME 45

CHAPTER 10: THE HONEYMOON 47

CHAPTER 11: A GOOD VALUE MAN 49

CHAPTER 12: LEVEL UP FLUID AND FREE 51

CHAPTER 13: 365 DAYS 53

ABOUT THE AUTHOR 55

Foreword

The stay-at-home order started in March 2020. Riots were instigated throughout the country, unemployment rates were at an all-time high, and working from home became normal during the pandemic, even for parents. It was a period of unusual stressors, chaotic events, and unknowns. All I wanted was to have fun with my hot and sexy girlfriends in Midtown. During the stay-at-home order, I spent a lot of time having Zoom parties and activities with my friends, which was nothing like meeting in person, though. I missed laughing out loud when we saw something funny, I missed the late-night parties and dancing in the streets.

My friends are good women. They are smart and take care of their business. Paris Baby has a super-hot body and is happily married with two kids. She enjoys working out. She is a woman who looks for validation within herself; it is a special quality she carries. Brie is a TikTok makeup influencer. She is always put together. Her hair and nails are always done to perfection. She is what I refer to as "The Prize." Her bank account is $180,000 but has a liability of $3,000,000. Living above her means, just for the recognition was how she lived her life. There is also Sage, who just can't seem to meet a good man. She wants the husband and the baby, and everything that comes with being married.

CHAPTER 1

THE STATE OF SINGLEHOOD

My name is Rhonda Wheeler. Yep, that's me on the cover. A Boss Babe with goals living single in Houston, a small business owner who lost her event planning company during the pandemic. I am trying to navigate through my new life, dating, reinventing myself, and finding Mr. JUST RIGHT, also known as HITMAN. They are attractive, hot, good-looking men who are high-income earners and very talented. I was married once in my twenties, but that was a disaster. My ex-husband was one of those parents that left. They say that parents will abandon their own children for many reasons. My ex-husband abandoned our two boys. It left me broken and confused. I couldn't understand how he could just leave them for me to raise. I assumed all the responsibilities, from daycare expenses to putting them through college. The responsibilities were overwhelming. We moved around a lot. I was trying to find a place of peace. The peace I was looking for would only come when I let go and moved on.

In my thirties, I dated around. I dated football players, businessmen, and real-estate investors. I guess I was trying to find a daddy figure for my two boys. Wealth is a magnet for most women. I am one of them. I am attracted to expensive cars, big houses, big incomes, and powerful status. They took good care of my children and I. We were always on vacation. I always had the latest bags, shoes, and clothes. That got old too, because wealthy men cheat. Women are hypergamous; they always date and mate up. In my forties, I'm looking for a serious relationship. I'm looking for a HITMAN. I mean just right in all the right places: personality, body, and American Express Black Card. But when did the world stop meeting in person? When did "we matched online" mean we are good for each other? Does that mean we are a couple? You are not the only one feeling the dating app blues. People at all ages are turning to dating sites to find love, which only leads to disappointment after disappointment. Which brings me to the questions: How do you find love today? Are people still looking to find love? Does love exist anymore?

CHAPTER 2

IT'S A MATCH

It's a Match! How do you find love today? Finding real love online is very challenging. Online dating sites and apps provide users with a large pool of prospective suitors behind a keyboard who pretend to be anyone they want to be. I believe people are still looking to find real love and not some creep behind a computer or cell phone. Not knowing how much is true and how much is fake can be very daunting and damaging. Love is something that you find. It can be in a person or thing. Love should no longer be blind; it should be open to getting your feelings hurt because love brings your heart into a relationship, and when the heart is in a relationship, there is always pain.

My first online dating experience was exciting. It was a Friday night. I set up my profile, gave them a little something to look at but not too much. I found nothing in the first ninety-nine swipes. My pointer finger went numb, so I went to bed. The next day, I repeated the same steps, but nothing. Nothing on the third day. On the fourth day, I got a match. "Let me say something nice to him." I sent him a message saying, "Good morning, my name is Rhonda." He never responded back.

This went on for three months of me swiping through pictures to have men not reply to my messages. I wasn't sure if I could survive another night as a single lady in the city that was shut down. By the fourth month, I closed my account, but before I deleted my profile, I took one more look at the dating pool. There he was; it started as a simple hello, and blossomed into this fantastical journey.

We were obsessed with one another, messaging regularly throughout the day, writing about being soulmates and creating an entire world in our joint imaginations. I fell very hard for him, and he did for me. Then it was time to move this from the phone to a real "in-person" meet-up.

The night before, I was so nervous and excited about meeting this man. We met at my favorite spot in Rice Village. He was tall, brown-chocolate, and had a masculine body. He was beyond toned muscle, well-built, visible through clothing. His muscles strain against his Samuganna fabric at the forearms, biceps, and chest. His dimples stood out whenever he would laugh. His teeth were professionally whitened. He smelled just like the Hermes store, and I had to call my ride-or-die. That night, I liked every photo he ever posted. The next day, we met again. He took me to a music and dance bistro where famous musicians got their start.

I was living in a fantasy world, and we were both ready to love. He made himself into what I wanted him to be, and vice versa. It was so good between us. The connection was so real, and he made me feel safe. It was good to be with a man who adored and cherished me.

This man had my heart, mind, and body. I can't explain how much time I invested in this man in such a short time. You see, it turns out that every man I've ever known has been a liar and just trash. His mama and his sisters knew that he was trash, but they kept defending them "fuckboys."

This was something new and special, and I wasn't ready to let it go. For you to understand my feelings for "HITMEN," you need to know about all the "fuckboys" who have staggered through my life over the past five years. It was disastrous. My girlfriends tell me the reason I've collected such a number of losers is because of my ridiculously high standards. Oh, not so. I like to think of my rules as "SOP" (Standard Operating Procedures). They are necessary for a busy mom who is over the BS.

Ladies, always keep what a guy "Must-Have" List. You deserve nothing more than, what? "Everything." Things I included in my "Man-Must-Have" List are really simple, ladies.

- » **Rule Number 1:** Good breath; get rid of that dead tooth. We aren't kissing, no stinky breath.
- » **Rule Number 2:** Must be taller than I am. I'm only 5'4", which shouldn't be too hard.
- » **Rule Number 3:** No braids, twists, or locks. Nope...Nope...Nope!
- » **Rule Number 4:** He must be older than me. I don't know why, I just need him to be older than me.
- » **Rule Number 5:** He must be educated. I have a degree. I need him to be degreed up too.
- » **Rule Number 6:** He must be able to dress well.
- » **Rule Number 7:** He must be able to cook something; I need to eat too.
- » **Rule Number 8:** He must be able to attain wealth. We both can't be broke at the same time.
- » **Rule Number 9:** He must smell good.
- » **Rule Number 10:** He must enjoy sex.
- » **Rule Number 11:** There should be a spiritual side to him.
- » **Rule 12–20** He can't be a womanizer, liar, cheater, disrespectful, broke, married, or absent from home.

Now, I've been known to deviate from the list every once in a while. I've recently concluded that the reason why my relationships with all these men didn't work out is because I created this "List." Why was this relationship rule-book created? One reason this rulebook was created is to give women more mandates to stress about. Another reason this rule book was created is to keep women single. That's just my opinion. But really, ladies, life is already stressful enough. We don't need to create rules to police and harass adult men.

I am not saying that you need to put up with his distrust. What I'm saying is, people are imperfect. You are uniquely created. True authenticity is the key to any successful relationship. If we are going to fulfill our ultimate goals, and purpose, there has got to be someone with whom we can be authentic. Ladies, that doesn't mean your mother, sister, and friends. We are going to have to practice being BFF with our lovers.

It seems like every wedding I've been to in the last few years has centered around the theme "today, I marry my best friend." If being friends with your lover wasn't the main theme, it was at least a subtheme or decoration or part of the toast. And every one of the couples was really invested in being best friends or becoming better friends in their relationship. Is it wrong to have your lover as your BFF? Well, it's important to get along and enjoy spending time together, but a bestie shouldn't come before your man. He is the only person you talk to about everything. Especially when it comes to venting about your best friend from college (who will absolutely get on your nerves at some point). While you certainly don't have to replace your current best friend with your partner, there are some things you can do to take your relationship friendship game to the next level. You're probably already doing some of these, but if not, no worries. It's never too late. Try including him in your morning workout routine. Also, you can try making funny TikTok videos together and go on adventures, try new things, and do actual activities like cooking on a regular basis.

CHAPTER 3

THE 3-DATE RULE

What is your ultimate goal? To be rich? To be happy? To have better habits? To be alone? Well, my ultimate goal is to find the perfect guy and fall in love with him. Wow! That sounds so cliché. Again, I want to find the perfect guy, who is hella sexy, makes six figures or more, is confident, and enjoys sex that lasts long. I am a single, divorced woman who meets a man on a dating app. A man who awakens my sexual longing for the first time, leaving me feeling helpless and breathless. "My backbones are still imprinted on the mattress, my walk is funny, my pelvic bone shifted somehow."

Third-date rule, inappropriate or appropriate? The first day we had sex was on our third date. Have you heard of the "3-date rule"? It is a dating rule which dictates that both parties withhold sex until at least the third date. Waiting until the third date or later supposedly gives a woman a better chance of keeping a man's interest, while it gives a man sex soon enough to keep his interest, without giving him sex so soon that he sees a woman as little more than a one-night stand. Yep, I gave up my recipe on our third date. And the fourth date...and the fifth date...sixth date and every date after.

The first time we had sex, our bodies were in the midst of being touched by the other sexual partner, while our minds were immersed in the sensations to think any thoughts at all. We were focusing completely on what's happening in the present moment. That night I experienced multi-orgasms all through the night, wanting the night to not end. For me, having pleasurable sex is everything. But with my new date in my life, sex feels like it is "on-demand." When he comes, it is far more interesting—and believable.

Every morning, after giving up my recipes, I would fix him a good old country breakfast with Southern shrimp and grits, Southwestern scrambled eggs, vegan maple bacon, and a venti flat dark coffee with oak milk. Soon, I was making his dinner, and then his lunch.

Being a single, beautiful entrepreneur and mother in her forties is not all voodoo or hoodoo. It's a sassy mix of spices. Dating should be fun, entertaining, and sex should be a part of your dating life. Date with a purpose in mind by figuring out what type of person you would consider dating. When you find this person, you should date by looking classy, sexy, and with a nurturing attitude.

I know what you're thinking. My life is busy too. Why isn't he bringing me food in bed? I love cooking and I plan events for a living—and I enjoy creating insanely difficult meals after a night of.... Well...you know!

The ultimate goal is to find someone that you like. Throw dating out the window. Start to enjoy your HITMAN, even if that means not liking everything about him at first. But if you work on it overtime, it will become simple. Life is short. EAT, SEX, AND DATE.

CHAPTER 4

HE CALLED

I know we can all relate to how important it is to us to have a man call after we have given up the recipe. Why men don't call after sex is beyond me. Ladies, we hold the power to control our own destiny. If your guy has not called you back after sex, leave him alone. Don't call him, don't text him. Delete him from all your social media accounts. You don't have to wait for a couple of days to go by before you remove him. Believe me, he is somewhere not thinking about you. No woman wants to feel used; no one wants to feel like a hit-quit to a guy that they have been seeking. No one still knows why a man will chase you, only to dump you after giving up your recipes.

Red flags can appear out of nowhere. Men can be tricky when they appear after you have been physically intimate. When I'm feeling down and out, I go into a protective mood by protecting my thoughts and emotions. I will start by quoting Bible scriptures. Amid chaos, I start claiming the "law of attraction." Ladies, we have the power to change our situation. We don't have to wait to be validated.

For the ladies who aren't looking for anything serious, maybe you want to date but without a commitment, or maybe you like friends with benefits, or maybe you just have a high sex drive and you like having multiple sex partners. Just so that we are clear, my ultimate goal is to date with a purpose. Not dating and sexing men, but to date a guy and be fulfilled.

HITMAN called. So, what if I gave it up after a few weeks of dating? Sex is a two-way street, as is the decision for two people to be together. Ladies, don't look at me strange. We have all been there before. We are all adults. Women lie to each other about how long they held out. Having casual sex is natural, while dating sex is intimate. As a result, the more time you spend with this person, the more your desire grows and you want to explore the physical, and a foundation for love is formed. When HITMAN called me the next day. I was so happy to hear from him.

From that day, we started dating exclusively. What happens next? If he wants a repeat of last night, then it shouldn't be an issue. Be real about the expectations. Tell the person your desires. Ask for a relationship, tell him that you're interested in dating only him. Ask him what he wants and listen to his side as well.

My passion is writing about love, sex, dating, and relationships. I write based on my own personal experiences and those that I relate to. I don't claim to have all the answers. I've dated a lot of men who aren't interested in a relationship. As a result, I ended up dating more and more men who weren't interested in a relationship. I do believe that a woman should date with a purpose in mind. Sometimes you meet people who have not healed from a previous relationship, which results in their bringing in unnecessary actions, or they might have seen bad examples. Either way, get out of the way. You can't fix them.

CHAPTER 5

MY RECIPES

I come from a family of chefs. My grandfather was a chef, my mother owned a bakery, my father makes a mean spice blend (my father wasn't always around. We have recently reconnected. I guess you can say that he was one of the fathers who left), and I enjoy cooking. I started watching my mother cook as a kid. My childhood memories include the smell of fresh baked breads, cookies, doughnuts, cakes, and pies. She never used a cookbook or measuring sticks. I had never helped my mother prepare a meal before. Her way of cooking was so robust, I could just taste every ingredient she used. In fact, her lasagna is my all-time favorite. Her kitchen was always filled with love, and she has inspired me to cook more at home with my kids. I believe food is what brings families together. Every day, dinner was served at seven p.m., and we ate as a family and shared our day's events.

My recipes are quick and easy-to-prepare recipes with amazing flavor from the author. You'll find great dishes for date nights, entertaining guests, and family meals. I share my recipes with you because there was a time I struggled with gestational diabetes from my first pregnancy. From there, I started getting serious about cooking when I realized I could keep this Dx for the rest of my life. After discovering I'm also gluten-free and battling stomach issues, I dove headfirst into making meals at home so I could eat healthy and feel satisfied. For my readers, I have compiled a list of my delicious meals for two or more. These are my recipes that got him coming back for more. I hope my recipes bring you pleasure and fulfillment. Thank you - Rhonda Wheeler

My One-Pot Meals

1. Firecracker Shrimp Dumpling Soup

» Add salt, pepper, Old Bay, creole, regular paprika, onion, garlic powder, thyme, cracked crushed peppers, bay leaves, and season to taste

- » 1 Large onion
- » 1 Green bell pepper
- » 3 Medium tomatoes
- » 3 Cups of vegetable stock
- » 4 Cloves garlic
- » 10 Strips of Open Kettle Dumplings
- » 6 Stalks celery
- » 2 lbs. Deveined shrimp
- » 1 Frozen mixed vegetable bag

2. TikTok Worthy Gumbo

» Add salt, pepper, Old Bay, creole, smoked paprika, onion, garlic powder, thyme, cracked crushed peppers, bay leaves, and season to taste/

- » 3 Cups of gumbo stock
- » 1 Pound chicken drumsticks, cooked
- » ¼ Cup of olive oil
- » 2–3 Ounces vegan andouille sausage
- » 2–3 Ounces vegan Italian sausage
- » 2 lbs. deveined shrimp
- » Crawfish (one pound)
- » Okra (one pound)
- » 1 Pound crab meat, lump
- » 4 Dungeness clusters
- » Serve it with white rice

3. Jambalaya Remix
Color Is Everything

» Add salt, pepper, Old Bay, creole, regular paprika, onion, garlic powder, thyme, cracked crushed peppers, bay leaves, and season to taste.

- » Add a box of Tony's Jambalaya Rice Box for an extra kick
- » 1 1¼ Large onion
- » 3 Cups of vegetable stock.
- » 1 Pound of cooked shrimp
- » Cup of olive oil
- » 1 Bag of fresh spinach
- » 1 Can of red kidney beans

4. Carnival Time Garlic Shrimp and Grits with Parmesan and Cheddar Cheese

---

» Add salt, Old Bay, pepper, creole, smoked paprika, onion, and garlic powder, add seasoning to taste.

- » 4 Vegan smoked maple bacon slices
- » 3 Cloves garlic
- » 1 Pound fresh shrimp
- » 1 Cup fine grits, uncooked
- » ½ Cup shredded cheddar cheese
- » ½ Cup queso white block Velveeta
- » ¼ Cup of parmesan cheese
- » 3 Tablespoon of salted butter
- » ¼ Olive oil
- » 4 Cups water

Garnish with green onions and parsley if desired

I had to hit him with the avocado toast.

5. Texas Roadhouse Avocado Grilled Cheese and Ham Baguette

» Add salt, Old Bay, pepper, creole, smoked paprika, onion, and garlic powder, add seasoning to taste/

- » 1 Avocado
- » 1 Slice of muenster cheeses
- » 3 Red potatoes fried in butter
- » 1 Loaf of French baguette
- » 2 Fried sunnyside cooked eggs
- » 2 Slices ham from the Black Forest

Spread one avocado over toasted baguettes and double layer it up with spicy mustard.

Garnish your plate with parsley.

6. All-time Favorite - Rodeo Steak and Eggs

» Add salt, Old Bay, pepper, creole, paprika, onion, and garlic powder seasoning to taste.

» Use the McCormick Blacken Steak package for the perfect color.

» 1 Small can mushroom sauce (keeps steak tinder)
» 1 Quarter-pound steak
» ½ Cup olive oil
» Cook on boil until your desired taste.
» Serve with two sunny-side-up eggs on the side.

Garnish with Italian flora and fauna.

7. Blow His Mind Three-Cheese Bacon Beyond Burger

» Add salt, Old Bay, pepper, creole, paprika, onion, and garlic powder, seasoning to taste

» 5 Pounds Beyond Burger meat package
» A Single avocado
» 3 Slices of vegan maple bacon
» 1 Tomato, ripe

Sauce up the buns with Chick-fil-A sauce. Instead of ketchup, use Sweet Baby Rays BBQ Sauce.

Serve on a warm sesame seed buttery toasted buns.

8. Endless Toss Salad - This is not your a verage Greek Salad.

- » 1 Whole salmon, skin left on for added crunch
- » 2 Tbsp. blackening seasoning
- » 1 Large bag of romaine salad mix
- » 6 Roma tomatoes (grape tomatoes are delicious too)
- » 3 Sliced cucumbers
- » 1 Large red onion
- » 1 Large green bell pepper
- » 1 Can black olive
- » 1 Cup feta cheese

Top with black peppercorns and add boiled eggs if desired.

9. Slammin' Cajun Garlic and Double Boiled Seafood Boil

» Add salt, Old Bay, pepper, creole, smoked paprika, onion, and garlic powder, seasoning to taste.

» 3 Sticks of butter
» 4 Garlic cloves
» 1 Can of beer
» 2 Pound lobster tail
» 2–3 Ounces vegan hot sausage
» 2–3 Ounces vegan Italian sausage
» 2 Pounds of deveined shrimp
» Crawfish (one pound)
» Okra (one pound)
» Crab cluster weighing 3 pounds
» 4 Potatoes, whole
» 4 Ears of sweet corn, serve it with white rice
» Spread hot butter seasoned with garlic sauce over the food.

Remove the pot from the boiler and spread butter and garlic sauce over the food until ready.

Garnish with Italian seasonings.

10. The Ultimate Feast: Fresh Blackened Whole Tilapia

» Add salt, Old Bay, pepper, creole, paprika, onion, and garlic powder, seasoning to taste.

» ½ Cup olive oil
» 1 Whole tilapia
» Boil until ready.

Garnish with all of his favorite dishes. Hot sausage and BBQ shredded beef.

11. Dessert Cozy Strawberry Shortcake

I'm not a huge dessert eater, but my favorite dessert to make is my homemade Strawberry Shortcake with sliced bananas and vanilla wafers.

- » Vanilla box cake with Very Strawberry Whip
- » 1 Package Betty Cracker Vanilla Cake box
- » 1 Pound fresh strawberries
- » 4 Bananas, ripe
- » 4 Cups of crushed vanilla wafers (about 120 wafers)
- » 12 Ounces of frozen whipped topping, thawed

Served chilled.

CHAPTER 6

SPICE THINGS UP

Growing up, I loved playing with Barbies. There is a study out there that says, "Barbie's message for girls is a narrow one." I have mixed feelings about that study. Playing with Barbies is how I discovered that my appearance is important. It is okay to be beautiful, successful, and confident. I have some great tips on how you can look good on a budget while dating.

My favorite go-to apps are Pinterest, TikTok, and YouTube, when I want to be inspired by something as simple as what to wear to dinner, how to set the table for "dinner for two," or how to look classy and sexy at the same time. Having the right look is important. Sometimes that look isn't always going to look good on you. The world is filled with images pressing women to be cornbread fed—can lead to depression, low self-esteem, and eating disorders, which all can have a negative impact on your life. Women will be judged on how they look rather than what they can do, which is unfortunate but true.

From stay-at-home dinners to nightlife, I always look pretty, sexy, and classy for my man. How do I do it? As I mentioned, my inspiration comes from experts in the industry. Being an event planner, I have a good idea of what not to do. Here are some helpful tips:

» Ladies, stop showing it all. I can't stress that anymore! Just stop!
» Classy, to me, is how you carry yourself. For instance, if you don't feel like you are a catch, you will talk yourself out of attracting a good value man.
» Energy is one of the "laws of attraction." Let your hot girl energy glow. I'm 5'4" and weigh 125 pounds, but everything does not look great on me because I'm not cornbread fed in all the right areas, so naturally, I pick what I like about my body the most and I focus on that.

Sexy is appealing to me. For instance, expand your vocabulary outside of reality TV. Be able to converse on different levels. Don't bore the man with all your degrees. We are living in a world where stripers can be millionaires, and bloggers influence the market. I try to meet the guy where he is. Just by asking him to share a great moment in his life.

The dining table sets the tone; think of it as how you want the evening to go. You will need great lighting. Try a variety of flameless candles to set the mood. I like to have some good music playing in the background. You can find fancy plates and glasses at your local Home Goods store.

Let me define a good man. According to Merriam-Webster, the meaning of "the good" is that part of someone that is kind, honest, generous, and helpful. A significant component of womanhood is understanding the importance of your worth. A man's role is to be all those things and more. If you have experienced a life of chaos in relationships, this message may be confusing.

A man may exhibit non-verbal communication and lack the opportunity to express his feelings or emotional attachment to you. According to Bradford Davis, "The Mental Health of Black Men": "In particular, black males have dealt with a significant amount of stress, overt forms of oppression, and trauma. For generations, the African American community has struggled to fight the consistent battle that has plagued black communities for centuries. Our survival in America has been a continuous struggle."

Having a good value man means having patience, which promotes a level of obedience. A man can learn over a period of time to give you what you need. However, obedience may also be easily broken by a change in circumstances.

As a woman, I have experienced ups and downs and highs and lows. I want a man to accept me in my moments. Ask yourself, are you a nurturer? Are you a runner when times get tough? Are you a wife? The ideal of having a healthy relationship is an ongoing process. Understanding how to have a positive outcome depends on you.

CHAPTER 7

THE CHANGE

We have all experienced change at some point. The change is when men start to distance themselves from you. The change usually happens around three to six months of dating. Dating is like an organ; it is forever changing. When the change comes, no one is warned. It's nothing you have done; it just randomly happens after dating. Many feel it's a man's way of pulling back when things are getting too serious. Some say it's more of a defense mechanism. I believe people will pull back from you for no reason. I feel that people will leave you without notice. I also believe if you want something, you shouldn't set it free.

Here are some tips I used when I felt the relationship change.

» Set personal boundaries. This will allow you to move freely and experience how you want people to treat you.
» Know your limits. This will allow you to move freely without stress.
» Know that you are in this together.
» Share your feelings. Let him know that it makes you uncomfortable when he is distancing himself.

- » Let him know that you're thinking about pulling away if things don't change.
- » If he is going through something, learn how to practice empathy.
- » Relationships are a serious matter. You should talk it through before making the decision to walk away.

The change will happen, and it will force you both to come to heads, but that is what relationships are all about: sharing a space with someone who can make you go crazy at any given moment. Setting personal boundaries is essential to a healthy relationship. They are guidelines, rules, or limits that a person creates to justify a safe space for them to function in.

Try to build a spiritual relationship to keep you grounded, but not necessarily in that order.

- » Family/Friends
- » Spirituality
- » Fun/Adventure
- » Finance
- » Health/Fitness
- » Education and Career

Again, my passion is writing about love, sex, dating, and relationships. As a disclaimer, I don't claim to have all the right answers. I write based on my own personal experiences and those that I relate to.

CHAPTER 8

EAT, SEX, and DATE

EAT: If it's not eating, then you're doing something wrong. No matter what stage your relationship is in, it is never too late to start cooking. Dining out is cool, and taking pictures for Instagram and TikTok is great. I promise you will feel so much better uploading pictures of your own dishes. One day, I decided to invite "HITMAN" over for dinner. I went to the grocery store the night before to buy some spices, salmon, crawfish, steak, and salad. I couldn't decide what to make, so I bought them all. I was so nervous, and my anxiety was kicking in—I can't quite explain why. This wasn't my first-time cooking. I've cooked for my ex-husband before. But this time it felt different. I felt confident about cooking with him, and it felt good to explore new and exciting dishes with him. Try making smart meals at home with your man. I know my way around the kitchen, so I recommend you start with my one-pot meal recipe. Take it from me: By starting simple and learning the rules before you break them, cooking can become a great source of joy in your life!

SEX: Throughout history, women have come up with funny names to describe their vaginas without saying the word "vagina." Somehow, over the years, women have associated their vaginas with food. Well, it is a delicious food. My top ten favorites are: The Cookie, Cream Puffs, Red Hot Wings, The Cherry, Hot Pot, French Fry Dip, Meat Curtains, Tacos, Fish and Lips, and Red Velvet Cake. Throughout my book, I use "My Recipes" as a term to describe sex. If you're dating a guy and you are thinking about making him wait for the "Cookies," this will work if your guy has very little to offer. But if your guy has it going on, chances are he will move on to taste another woman's "Recipes." According to "The law of social exchange theory," it states that "no relationship can stay out of balance for too long. High-valued men who are better off, are less likely to wait and accept those unbalanced relationships."

DATE: For ladies who aren't looking for anything serious, maybe you want to date but without a commitment. Or maybe you like friends with benefits. Or maybe you just have a high sex drive and you like having multiple sex partners. Just so that we are clear, my ultimate goal is to date with a purpose. Not dating, sexing, and sampling another man's recipe, but to date a guy and be fulfilled.

CHAPTER 9

SAY MY NAME

I can recall the first time he said, "Rhonda, I love you." It was during mind-blowing sex. I'm not sure if that counts. When I met his family and friends, I thought, *wow, this guy is serious.* How important is it for a man to let others know about you? "Say my name, say my name" song recording artist Beyonce thought that it was so important, she even wrote a song about it. During the getting-to-know stage, you should never assume that a person is single. He/she could be juggling multiple people and just haven't met that one, yet.

The joke goes somehow like "Every man needs a good woman in his life, a woman who is beautiful, a woman who is sociable, a woman who can cook, and a woman who's good in bed. But most of all, he needs to make sure these women never meet." The assumption is, if a man hasn't introduced you to any of his friends and family, he is hiding you because he is embarrassed or ashamed about it, or both, or he wants to keep his options open.

I think if you are dating exclusively, it doesn't mean something is going on. He could have his reasons, such as maybe he's had multiple failed relation-ships, and he thinks that you're an awesome person, but he isn't sure about some of the snarky comments you make whenever he mentions having a future together. If you've shown any indication of flip-flopping about being in a long-term committed relationship, he might just think it's best to keep you out of the spotlight for a while until he is sure you're not going to dump him when things aren't good.

There could be a million different reasons why he doesn't want others to meet you—I'm not saying if you have been in an exclusive relationship for longer than six months, and you never met any of his friends and family. You should just take his word for it. You teach people how to treat you and don't tolerate bad behaviors. Consider all the other reasons before you're prepared to make accusations. My suggestion is for you to lose the strong black woman cliché. Even Jesus required help from all his disciples. Learn how to be vulnerable, nurturing, and passive.

According to an article by *Ebony*, "How the Strong Black Woman Kills Love," the "strong black woman" or "angry black woman" stereotype has stood the test of time. Several depictions of stubborn, argumentative, bitter black women continue to dominate television airwaves, and the idea that we are difficult to get along with is pushed to the forefront on all platforms. Ebony defines "strong black women" as, in the general sense, the strong (angry) black woman is believed to be so powerful that she does not need a man or partner to get things done. She's eager to work five jobs, take care of her household, and raise kids all on her own. She always defies the odds and isn't afraid to tell a man that she can do it all by herself. In fact, she's so #teamunbothered and independent that she doesn't even need validation or any type of appreciation from her significant other (if she chooses to have one). Essentially, she is Superwoman. Instead of a cape, she has melanin and is tasked with cleaning up the messes of everyone around her.

Whenever I think about black heterosexual relationships, I often wonder if many people are aware of the negative effects of the term when it comes to love, romance, and true partnership. Have we actually taken the time to consider just how damaging the "strong (angry) black woman" stereotype is?

CHAPTER 10

The Honeymoon

This feeling of euphoria. We were both feeling very attached, passionate, and happy with the relationship. Thinking about the other person constantly, wanting to be around each other all the time, and lots of physical or sexual attraction. The relationship was filled with a lot of excitement, energy, and romance. I can remember when my feelings started to shift. I thought about it all the time. I let things slide because I thought if I brought it up, I would see the real him. I let it interrupt my sleep, I didn't want to eat, I avoided talking to him for extended periods of time because I wasn't ready to leave my honeymoon. I wanted to live in this space forever.

I saw stars, fireworks, and I was wearing the perfect iconic wedding dress. This is called the honeymoon phase and can last anywhere from two months to two years. The length of time a couple spends in this phase varies significantly depending on the way the relationship starts, what's going on in the couple's lives, the partners' personality traits, how long it takes to fall in love, and other factors. This phase can be challenging, but it is your job to see it to the end. Now you get to ask yourself, "Is this somebody I can spend time with? Is this somebody I still enjoy? Is this a person I can still laugh with?"

Setting Boundaries and Communication is key. If your man is dismissive of your feelings, thoughts, and concerns. If he plays the blame game, twists conversation, and cuts you off in the middle of your conversations to avoid him accepting responsibility. GET OUT! Does he make you feel angry or mad over and over again? GET OUT! It is a true character flaw. A man should emulate the three Ps (Profess, Provide, Protect). Don't be afraid to check in with your partner about things that might be bothering or worrying you. In order to be on the same page, it's important that you meet them where they are emotionally and give them the opportunity to work together on what you both need.

CHAPTER 11

A Good Value Man

One who has a purpose in life. One who is afraid of loosing everything if he isnt careful about his choices and who he spends his time with. One who is connected to his partner purpose, have a set of values and a desire to please his partner through reckoning, making improvements, and understands his successes, and works co-partnering by demonstrating good personal values to his partner He is not afraid to lose so his partner can win. Must bring to the table his heart, honesty, vulnerabilities, respect, compromise, intimacy, love, commitment, time and willingness.